In My Feelins

Cedric Till— 12/20/19

In My Feelins

Poems by Cedric Tillman

Word Poetry

Alex!

Thank you for your support! It's great to hear from you. I am ashamed to say I've had your novel all these years and haven't gotten to it! It will happen. (Also Lisa Schamess' book.) Would love to get your candid take on this as I take on some pretty thorny stuff here. I'm so grateful for my old classmates' support — its been really humbling. I pray all is well— Cedric

Published by Word Poetry
P.O. Box 541106
Cincinnati, OH 45254-1106

ISBN: 9781625493330

Poetry Editor: Kevin Walzer
Business Editor: Lori Jareo

Visit us on the web at www.wordpoetrybooks.com

Acknowledgements

Thankful acknowledgement is given to the following journals in which earlier versions of the poems below first appeared.

"The Legend of Famous Jameis," "Predestination," and "Sunset in Huntersville" appear in *The 100-Year-House Anthology,* Cherry Castle Books.

"Sundays on Rosehaven," "who needs 'im," and "Luxury" appear in *Apogee,* the literary magazine of High Point University.

"Bad Haiku Workshop," "PrEP," and "Safe Space" appear in *Barzakh Magazine.*

"Cankerworms" is forthcoming in *Furious Flower: Seeding the Future of African-American Poetry.*

"Tread on Me" appears in the anthology *Hand in Hand: Poets Respond to Race.*

"light reading" appears on the website of the HIV Here & Now Project (www.hivhereandnow.com).

"spontaneous generation" appears in *Iodine Poetry Journal.*

"respectability" appears in *The Manhattanville Review.*

"Relics" appears as "Push Me Away (Your Wedding Day)" in *The Men's Heartbreak Anthology.*

"Esoterica" and "Trust" appear in *The Pierian Literary Journal.*

"Supremacy, or The Black Lifestyle" appears in *Pleiades.*

"the flag" appears in *Rove.*

In My Feelins

Love Changes

Creative Tension

Windsor Park (Welcome to Charlotte East)

Notes

"I am only concerned with letting people see the truth of our lives…we must bring things out into the open. There are some people you can't reach. You neutralize this kind…" – Godfrey Cambridge

"As human beings, we wanna connect, we wanna be together and sometimes we're afraid that whatever we think or whatever we have to say might separate us from the community or those we would want to belong to and the effect is that…you know, we can silence ourselves, we can hold back…very important thoughts, very important things that…should be contributed. We all should contribute to this society. And I think that poetry offers a place to name what should be named, or to speak thoughts that we may be afraid to speak…" -Ruth Forman

"In line with my conviction that of utmost importance these days is serious discussion and the winning of new allies to the struggle…there is too much to be done on the grassroots level, too much education needed on the essence and strategy of the movement for us to waste time with demagoguery, no matter how appealing it might be." – Bayard Rustin

big booty, better thighs/I ain't wanna tell her bye – T.I.

"Boy when white folks come see you you successful boy, you somebody!" – Bernie Mac

"Your words are hardly designed to produce the kind of consensus and understanding the book wants to produce." – Andrew Neil

"…needs to be the person that is helping to weave together the alliances to build the kind of majoritarian movement that we need in order to win." – Bill Fletcher, Jr.

My days left here may not be long/I wouldn't waste my time tellin' you nothin' wrong – Betty Wright, "No Pain, No Gain"

"When it seems like people are voting against their interests, I have probably failed to understand their interests." – Chris Ladd

My feelings can't control my destiny. – Tamela Mann, "God Provides"

Love Changes

pretending to twerk

you are
a story I'm up not telling

a game I'm up watching
from a change.

a secret I won't share,
some truth I keep private
got you bound. that close.

I am

a drowsy bathroom trip
from good rest.

a night on my stomach out
from good sleep.

something I must learn to asphyxiate
from a promotion.

I am

tunnel vision away
from good husband,

20 pounds from BMI nirvana,

a few thousand swings
of a kettlebell.

As I live,
I hold in the bowl of curve
below my navel

like an ordinary me.

luh' friends (for Beatrice)

ever since I met ya/I could peep the pressure - Tupac, "Can U Get Away"

you know I ain't mess w/you 'cause of yo' friends
wouldn't have you caught slummin'
know you hood 'cause you said

I look the same
and I said
you look the same

and I said "*it don't crack, do it?*
and you said "*Uh, OKAY?*"

that's that thing right there

would love to take you somewhere we could be ignant as hell
make jokes out loud you just 'sposed to text or email
ones you message but don't post on Facebook
send you back to yo' luh friends

yo luh' fancy friends
that work for nonprofits
and foundations and colleges and shit

not that I can't talk fancy too
I can use terms like *microaggression*
and *heterosexist* in sentences for you

but I'm country
I'm bound to slip that Bogalusa Opalocka Anson County in
liable to be where the Baptist church and the fatback at

come ride yo' fine ass out for a minute
just me and you

dissertation committee ain't gotta know you like Boosie

come be whoever you was 'fore you came up here for like five minutes
come get this dinner so I can send you back
'fore they find out you AWOL wit' the riffraff

yo' luh' friends

Relics

don't you know these dreams/I wish could be/the real you and me -The Jacksons, "Push Me Away"

we were here for the memoir
as much as the love
you knew I would take notes
on the taste of your totems

crimson-winged butterflies and a headdress
their meanings disclosed
in a haunt of incense.

how soon can I make peace
with the dark thick curls
that litter this bedroom like relics,
reminders of worship and exile?

getback

It's like that girl a couple buildings down you'd loved for years
the one you'd come out on the stoop for shirtless
for no reason except weight training

having seen her emerge during surveillance on her doorway
from the perch of your bedroom window

for whom you had feigned coincidence
in search of applause
A *You've been working out–*

Though you were always the dude
she clicked over to dude on

commercial break filler
for *Video Soul.*

And later, after you'd
filled out nice,
when she'd become whitened and dwarfed

The invite went out
though the party was over.
You showed just to settle a score.

Distraction (Harmony, in red)

Hale, opulent thighs
Half-moon into the hem of a garment
Steeped in red—
Curls lambent in lemon chiffon
The crimson blot contrast of lipstick

An aureole of décolletage
Conspire against level-best eyes.
She worries his mack game,
Bedevils his righteousness,
Blood-rushes a whisky
Of wonder.

loitering

when she asks if you were looking at her ass
you should always be able to say *no*
with conviction, even if you're lying.
experienced eyes never linger.

if she's honest wit' her own self she'll concede
petite white woman in the loose black tank
and zebra-striped tights
is thicker in the thighs than normal.

no, you were not looking at her ass,
having long since turned your attention
to her matching black toenail polish,
these fly leather thong sandals she got on, and

check those out honey,
ain't they cute, you like them?

for the nude

1.

Her slightly parted legs loom over the floor,
artificial light revealing their isosceles undulation,
the musculature protracted for our measure
as she stares an assertion over our heads
into an expedient brick.
Though the A-line is draped over a gym bag
near an easel in the corner,
an invitation to sketch out
whatever secrets are brought to mind,
I train my attention obliquely.

2.

Tipped in pink,
the brooding stigmata of birthmark
thrived at the pulse in her fingers,
their doleful umbrage
attending a sunset
that cinctured her hips.

Tea

Now of course,
you take it how you wanna take it
But I like that black pekoe, that's good stuff.
Some like it creamed to a burnt orange brink,
or tinged with a jot o' milk

Had it like that too—it's all to the good.
Steep it five minutes, lil' sugar
Let that thang sit a 'lil sump'n 'fore you sip it
and you got a sweet, murky concoction.

Now once you get accustomed,
it's a pain to cut back—
'Cause without that caffeine,
you might just nod off.
See I like a little kick,

an encouraging prod
like a slowed-up slap hand
'fore it reaches the face.

ass

a turn of the wrist
into the dip of a palm over the rise,
like a fitting
says all night like this
won't do.

dark side of the hand
circling, pleading
come put us to sleep.
take the pill or find
a futon. the tortured
stroke of nails
over this side of the world

is rounded and firm
as asses go,
skin soft under the skin
over the bones in my fingers
like powdered sugar.

Spew.

...These things saith the Amen...the beginning of the creation of God; I know thy works, that thou art neither cold nor hot: I would thou wert cold or hot. So then because thou art lukewarm, and neither cold nor hot, I will spue thee out of my mouth. - Revelations 3:14-16 (KJV)

Lord I know my secular-to-gospel CD ratio is 30:1—I plead the blood over that Easter Sunday service during which I drifted off into a mix of "Great Is Thy Faithfulness" with "Come to Me" by Diddy and fine-ass Nicole, see if you slow down "Faithfulness" just so, you

can be spewed. I know Lord.

I hope the person who put "jerk chicken and salad" under that picture of Serena and the white girl is spewed for their humor if I am spewed for my laughter.

(And Robin is lost without you Paula-spew whoever Thicke wit' now.)

Spew for the Junior Johnson moonshine on top of the KJV in the floor of my Jeep.

Spew for how that Bible stays in the car all week.

Spew for the bachelor party and the lap dances with Daddy's insurance money minus spew for how I left early since it was my Sunday with the first graders—I know I need you Father, don't spew me, I'll surrender all, I won't be ashamed of you before men, I'm coming down right after this party for my 40th where the old-school stations do live broadcasts on Saturday-I'll be down at Savoy

or Vibrations

or Press Box

but right after Stacey done spinning I'll be down there Lord

yet one more time let mine eyes behold the women
fragrant and fastidious over their chicken wings at the bar in them stilettos
then right off to seminary at Belmont Abbey
I promise Lord, I'll put my hand to your plow

don't spew me for making love to that Jason Nelson song
the premarital shifting of atmospheres
the woman I tripped sensors with in the bathroom at the club,

Lord honor with your mercy the moderation with which I indulged
when I confessed that thang to my Christian Brothers.

colony, or my side of the bed

my husband makes of my body an oracle
every night reaching for truth
prognostications he's heard
when I'm too tired to speak

when I would rather lie

he will keen his shift
for so much as a whisper
even if he deserves silence
or screaming

will ply my breasts
my naked hips and thighs
make of my nature against the sheets
a longing an inquest.

My daughters jab at the soft rills
stretched along the border of my panties
I cannot tell if they are imagining their futures
or hungry for power

and on the way to lunch
men leer from the auto shop.
All day long I am bracing
for the laying on of hands

the missionaries

the one about Michael

suddenly I think of the dreadlocks
and their mannered confusion
abrading my fingertips,
of how principle kept me close,
a stay against flinching.

In the moment, one is distracted
by the clock in one's head
I don't notice his beard
though it may have skirmished my skin
on the lean in

I do note the languor in his shuffle
could not presage
the yielding in his shoulders
the molten surprise of curve
in his spine

I like to think the tension in my arms
meant to convey to his rib cage
a provisional surrender
isn't preconceived
that no love is lost, surely

surely he understands
in those counts and beats
I will recover my hands
lest they prattle behind his back
like comfort.

PrEP

I tell the doctor I lost my dad and five uncles to heart disease. He says I should change my diet, that he knows it won't be easy, but I could do it. He gives me this look and a piece of paper with the "Mediterranean food triangle" on it, then another filled with dire stats, his way of saying *do better.*

The holy roller vegetarians, sanctimonious vegans, lukewarm pescatarians—all thinking not doing something will save them. I like cabbage and collards but not like I like salt and bacon and red meat, so I take the BP meds and simvastatin. I call it compromise.

Doc is supposed to tell me I can change—I know it's his job. But it's been a few years now since I started seeing him, and I think we're kinda figuring that I won't.

Predestination

"For I know the plans I have for you," declares the Lord, plans to prosper you and not to harm you, plans to give you hope and a future...for whom He foreknew, He also predestined to be conformed to the image of His Son...- Jeremiah 29:11, Romans 8:28-32

We duel in verse, two country boys
with *big meetins* and choirs in common.
Over lunch he speaks of his authentic self,
of living in His spirit

and loving in his truth.
I tell him I want him to have life
and to have it abundantly,
that authenticity nearly cost me a wife,
and he laughs.
His laugh
matters.

He says ever since he was old enough
to know anything, he's known who he was

Which means God
meant the pill bottle on his nightstand
to be a lifeline,
so I don't believe him.

not my will

And he said, Abba, Father, all things are possible unto thee; take away this cup from me: nevertheless not what I will, but what thou wilt…the spirit truly is ready, but the flesh is weak.
– Mark 14:36-38 (KJV)

There's an adultery gene out now
but she won't buy it, she's anti-science
Act up and I can get the hell on,
me and all my hormones.
I'm Mr. Family Man on the computer,
You can tell when I talk I'm in church
and not just at Easter,

but I've known what I am
ever since fourth grade,
that summer in the apartments
when my white girl
found out about my black girl,
made me choose
while "where do broken hearts go"
played from a balcony across the street
like theme music.

There was always the urge
even after the extra mouth to feed
order and comfort
were no salve for the need
'Cause you're always an addict,
it's true.
But I wanna hold up a family portrait
like a black fist
from the lonely soapbox of my doorstep

in honor of our masquerades,
for how they are more useful
than so many truths we tell,
and let the revolution be a balm
for bad memories,
an asylum against fantasy.

trust

you like my body over yours at night
warm as a grandmother's handiwork
mingled bands
cross-purposed   even-hemmed
pedal-patterned into tartan designs
even as she runs her fingers over the errors,
gently back and forth
as if they could be rubbed out.

when I am away,
I know there is more of me in the shadow
than in the sunlight.
to hear me pray aloud
is to hear a prayer for a left hand
traced so perfectly close by a right
that it chafes each finger,
permanent ink dragged
down the shaft of my thumb
until I am what I say I am.

Creative Tension

Poetry Thug: kill nuttin' let nuttin' die (after Mobb Deep)

yo word is bond son, these bitch ass poets out here man, swear they got lines, poets swear they got stanzas and shit, poets ain't really hitting on shit son, poets is mad lame, poets is straight booty out here son, for real yo poets is straight full of shit my poet, these bobo ass pantoums poets be writing, ol goddamn, desiccated ass tankas and shit poets be writing

ay my poet, check this shit my poet, yo, poets be out here posting on the 'book, shit be like "oh, a poet was a semifinalist in bumfuck journal of new england," um, um, "poet got new joints up at 'poet that met me at the reading published me 'cause we went to the same mfa'.com'" ass poets out here man killin' me out here wit' that shit

posting yo' close but no cigar ass placings in every poetry group you in on the 'book poet, poets ain't really not trying to hear that shit

poet first of all, first of all if poets you know out here postin' and tweeting' and tumblin' and redditin' yo' shit poet you not hot poet, poets 'posed to be posting yo shit even if they don't know you son, poets be out here on the 'book like "yeah, yeah, yeah, I'mma, I'mma post this shit, kiss his ass then you know he might put me down in that reading series he got, he gone spit me a hot, indecipherable, arcane fuck outta here wit' that bullshit poet" ass blurb when I tag him in that shit

then poets be on that respectability shit and ain't even blow up yet, like, you know, like, get a name poet 'fore you go all "all lives matter" on us poet, you know what I mean, like, get a few awards poet, get in a masthead somewhere so I know to kiss yo' ass and defend the foul shit you did in your life in case I need you to look out for me, know what I'm saying, be heavy in the game before you take controversial stands poet for real, and real talk if you ain't challenging the cisheteronormative ableists out here kill ya self poet, it's time out for that shit, straight facts no printer my poet decolonize your mind you no *ashe*-sayin' muhfucka

and if you come at me with that church negro shit, some ol' MLK over Assata-type, tone-policed, pro-Israel no-fly zone in Syria-type Charles Rowell over Amiri Baraka-type shit, word is bond poet I'm shunning yo ass when I see you at the reading my poet, that's on my momma, I'm not looking up from my tofu when you walk in son, if I'm smoking my Newport outside the venue poet I'm not fuckin' talking to you poet, we not cool my poet, I give a shit if you featuring my poet, I'm not sitting close to you yo and God forbid poet I ever retweeted any shit of yours you ever wrote cause I'mma unretweet that shit, you gone see one less "like" on yo' pinned tweet poet, you feel me? The fuck outta here w/that bullshit.

Safe Space

nobody's safe in the fast pace of the rap race/ So keep your hoodies on/ and your boots laced/ Now I'm out, beaming back to the boondocks/ Nobody's safe chump, so keep your doors locked – EPMD, "Nobody's Safe Chump"

Like you, I like a little safe space. I don't like what's beyond the comfort zone. Sometimes, I'm spaced uncomfortably by zone safety. There's too much flyover country. Knowing people from flyover country can be unsafe. Even in cities, flyover country can start within a mile of the main drag. In the cities, the breweries, dog bars, and cupcake shops mean change done come.

It's not safe to hold a grudge too long. One sign you're in an unsafe place is a Confederate flag anywhere outside of a museum or a Lil' Jon sleeveless T. It's not safe to hold grudges against people who, despite other shortcomings, at least understand why you hold a grudge. People who believe your version of history are safer. It's unsafe for history to have versions.

People who don't know history are unsafe. People who know history and pretend it doesn't affect the present are very unsafe. People who don't carry history with them into voting booths are unsafe.

I never feel I'm in a safe space so I always pray. I always triple-check the screen doors and the sliding doors because I don't feel safe.

I want to feel safe but I don't feel safe because I don't know what I've done to deserve safety.

Lots of people more virtuous than me don't feel safe.

I always expect to feel unsafe in Walmart and McDonald's, but I go because I'm financially unsafe. Actually McDonalds' fries make me feel safe, though the burgers don't. I always feel safe at Ruth's Chris and want to feel safe there more often.

Do you know The Clipse, or Philly's Most Wanted, or N.O.R.E.? Who would win a safe space contest between Pharrell and Kim Burrell? Where did Skateboard go to get happy? Now where'd he get that joy? You can't tell who's pro-safety by who a talk show host uninvites, though one can learn what's safe to say from the experience. Kim makes me feel "safe in His arms"–some call this delusion, but it is delusion that makes me willing to risk safety. I don't have any Kim Burrell albums but I helped Pharrell move this dope for 15 years. I feel complicit in creating the lack of safety I need her to sing to me about getting from my delusion.

Popularity ain't safe.

White famous ain't safe.

People who expect safety are unsafe. Maybe my kids could go to a Christian school, a safe space. Go ye therefore and proselytize each other in safety. Behold, I send you out as lambs among other lambs.

People who think they can't change are too safe. People who think people can't change are unsafe.

The Neptunes produced "Use Your Heart" by SWV, which is my jurnt. If loving this song could make me safe, I'd be safe.

Barack and Michelle are never in safe space but they are in safer space now.

Marriage is safe.

George Zimmerman ain't safe, and George Zimmerman ain't safe.

When I say we disagree, I mean that whatever you come from that makes you different from me makes you dangerous. The fact that we disagree is my critique of your upbringing — in effect, you are upset about an environment that was imposed upon me. Without our differences, we see eye to eye.

How can I make you agree with me to make you safer? If you persist in disagreeing with me I will continue to mark you unsafe in my roll. Don't make me unfriend you.

Being wrong is profoundly unsafe.

Not calling out wrong is unsafe.

Calling out wrong is unsafe.

Facts are unsafe.

All presidents are unsafe to somebody.
One president is unsafe for everybody.

Liars are unsafe.

In a contest between very unsafe and unsafe, vote unsafe. Every time.

Yea, verily I say unto thee
Senility is unsafe, and dementia is unsafe,
but few things are unsafe
like a lack of home training.

Now the solar panels in the White House ain't safe. The Easter egg roll ain't safe. Michelle's garden ain't safe.

The womb is unsafe,
the birth is unsafe,
the sowing, unsafe
the reaping, unsafe.

Your chocolate lab: safe
The dog walking you: unsafe.

To make you feel safe I take off my shades,
say "excuse me" to you
when you need to be saying
"excuse me" to me in the aisle.

I was safe in the interview
but watch how I act when I get in the house,
how I renege.

SHHHAFE!!

[I never felt safer than when I was in my daddy's arms and I think people that never felt safe that way are more likely to be unsafe when they get older.]

Brother, she can be opened. She is unsafe. Sister, he wants to open you. He is unsafe. Brother, he wants to open you. He is unsafe. Sister, she wants to open you. She is unsafe.

Desire is unsafe.

Guns are unsafe. So many dangerous people,
so many safeties off.
In America, the people most likely to own guns
are the safest people in America.

People who don't want to make people safer are unsafe.
Having fewer children is inevitable once you get to a certain safety level.
It's not safe, the religion where you can't leave things to God when you've lost a fight.

Comparatively speaking, campus is always a safe space.

The first day of workshop
the professor proclaimed it a safe space.
Later, the professor said we were evangelists,
that the real work
was beyond our comfort zones.
I think the real work won't mind
if I make nice and graduate first,
just to be safe.

The Best I Can Do (for Keri)

I cannot count how many times
I wanted to kick you
for being full of shih zhu,
the constant peeing in our bedroom,
all the pinholes you nipped into Bojangles' breasts
and the fingertips of beloved children
with those baneful little scythes.

(your moodiness unnerved me —
a doleful look, and it seemed
you divined my ruminations of revenge
even at this distance in sentience)

Still you sidle up to me on the couch
needy for attention, as if your maniacal barking
at everyone approaching the door to leave
has earned you the right—
why the snuggling, as if things are cool,
like we have none of that history,
as if by now I don't know who you are?

It isn't that I wish you ill fortune
(so much as that you are something
I could do without, your lack of humanity
being too common a thing nowadays to long for)

Please know I was joking
when I said the best line
in Ice Cube's "Today Was A Good Day"
was "no barking from the dog."
I know people who love me
love you too. Surely there are future endeavors
I could wish you the best in, given a list.

Pirates (after Kevin Williamson)

it's ok. I mean, you just gotta, you know, figure it out. I mean, all this rancor over stuff. I mean, look, this is America. you can do anything. the ppl in the streets, I mean, yeah but it's really much ado about nothing. I mean, but I mean, look. I'm really annoyed,

take offense to this humanity thing. choices get made, the humans humanity works for are also making choices for humanity. what about them. this is about economics, not humanity. humanity is a meaningless word.

this is about which constituency is gonna get served. I know what happened. it's not happening now though. there are tradeoffs. 1100 families per day torn up. I mean, look, you tear up families when you send people to jail. you gotta enforce the law.

hey, you can do anything. they'll still be able to buy 'em. they'll just go into the parking lot and do the deal. it'll still go on. it makes people feel good to know a deal got made in Congress.

Person-to-person sales remain unregulated. It doesn't matter.

I don't think this makes much difference at all given current practice. this seems to be a total non-issue. this is absolutely meaningless.

what do we get on our side? the ATF sucks. the ATF is irresponsible and reckless. they are the country's worst law enforcement organization. I'm glad they're putting shackles on what they can access as far as records. I'm glad someone's putting some teeth into what they can and can't do.

it's a media creation, the gun coalition. a bunch of mayors. most of the votes are in the two big cities in the state. that's what this is about. I don't think people really care about this.

the million-mom march didn't do anything. the energy's been on our side since then. why don't people enforce the current law? we believe in putting people in jail for handgun violations. meet us there. the 90 percent really care about that.

this isn't about Hispanics. it's about their votes. business interests want this, Republicans think they need Hispanics. it's not a big issue. have these people been to the border? no way they're gonna catch nine of ten of these guys. They'll make up numbers. It's like test scores in Atlanta.

Look, you and I both know I know as much as any liberal with a piercing. I have a bald head and two earrings, when I deadpan you know I know what I'm talking about. Arrgh.

hell you say (after Khujo Goodie)

I see the puritanical fundamentalist right-wing running roughshod over new norms and black bodies. It's problematic by which I mean it's fucked up but I'm up for tenure and this is TV, not Facebook. I teach a queer studies course at IaintU—the first two weeks we talk about Jesus' disciples (I mean, come on, right?) and rap videos featuring posses from the early '90s. In grad school, a macroaggressive professor and I got into it over affirmative action and he took to calling me Pitchfork, some redneck—got A's in those classes but I should've had the BSU hold a vigil on the quad, put that activity fee to cardstock-quality flyer work. There's this sort of way in which one uses language to secure agreement without completely making the case right, I mean am I actually right or am I claiming I've made the case before I've made a case by way of inflection. Of course it's moral-I just said it was progressive. Liberal vs. conservative, women's health care vs. pro-life—really they're false dichotomies, to the extent that the latter, in each of those preceding dichotomies, is quite false. Your rhetoric is divizzive. *Divisive?* Divizzive. Get an advanced degree. And drop that country-ass pronunciation of harrisment, it's problematic. Our ability to euphemize supersedes the other side's. We don't want to fall into this really sort of abject apathy whereby we effectively mistake toleration for tolerance. It can't be tolerated. All opinions will be peer-reviewed. I think we'd all agree on that. Raise your hand if you disagree. The I has it.
*

You know, and let's talk about breathing, right, because there's this way in which it's become sort a trope, right, you know, something we do because we have to, insofar as we need to live. And it's very patriarchal, I think, in its way, breathing I mean, and I hope I live long enough to see people moving beyond the traditional respiration model to perhaps an older, less oppressive one, one more like…osmosis, you know, I really see us hurtling headlong into an era several million years of evolution away and to be clear, we're talking paradigm shifts the size of Ferris and not hamster wheels, let me just tell you. I go into more detail in my weekly "Woke Up Like…Diss" column for Huff Po—but I think we need to speak into the silences and create safe spaces to push back against this critique that's out there that says we're out of touch which I wholeheartedly disagree with, this really sort of devastatingly insidious idea that I, as some have alleged, personify such a caricature beyond a shadow of a doubt.
*

You know, really as long as it's not puritanical fundamentalist patriarchal Amish churchy—you could slap my momma. There may be some value in these ideological orientations, it's just that some other PhD, maybe one from Liberty or Wheaton or Grove City can go looking for it while I get tenure at a school whose professors actually appear on NPR and MSNBC. As my partner (*wife?*) PART-NER likes to say, more marriage, fewer guns. "Hello? Ride-sharing? Meet me at the intersectionality of...4 White Man and Euphemism, yes, I'm, I'm bringing my gender and some skin color—but don't come for me if you can't come for us." I'd tell you why you're wrong, but time is money and well—your factory's closed. Your intuitive value judgment is in conflict with my intuitive value judgment and there's absolutely no excuse for you people to be products of this environment. I take offense to the notion that I've predetermined a conclusion without data but with all due respect I know what I'm looking for. A bigot is *a person who strongly and unfairly dislikes other people and ideas, someone who's obstinate or intolerant in devotion to his or her own opinions and prejudices*. I'm agnostic of course, but there but for the grace of little g "god"— go I.

The Legend of Famous Jameis

In one version, when the cops pull him over
Jameis hops out with his hands all in his waistband.
But we just talking crab legs,
and Jameis silly. The cop understands,

figures a kid this talented
could only be going for his nuts,
hated he even had to file a report.
A second account has Jameis coming so close

he strokes the officer's beard
with a claw poking through the plastic wrap
and is literally smacked on the wrist.
In a third version,

they say Jameis walked his ol' country good ball playin'
socks and flip-flopped ass out that Publix in T-town
to a car he'd parked longways in handicapped,
where a quadriplegic veteran
had offered him the spaces.

He drives like he's juking DB's
and when he's finally stopped,
having skidded into a dusty patch of road shoulder
like he's stealing a base,

he hops out with the crab legs in the air.
The cop, who is white, and mortal,
tells him to stop right there son
but Jameis don't stop,

he's wearing his FSU sweatshirt
which allows him to pass,
collect $2 million dollars the first year.
The gun barrel plunges, a scepter extended

toward the high value target,
so Jameis gets right in the cop's face,
leans into an ear and coos
"Fuck me in the pussy.
I forgot to pay."

Tread on Me

We had the funeral for my freedom last night.
The right to life was 19 years old.
Freedom pulled a trigger and killed my freedom
because freedom trumps my freedom, is more precious
than my freedom.
My freedom died for your freedom,
didn't enlist but it died for this country, by this country.
Guns don't kill freedom, freedom kills freedom.

The other day the city said I could watch my freedom bleed out real cheap
Said they'd borrow some money to help me see my freedom bleed out in
broadband
but freedom sued the city,
said I didn't have that kind of freedom.
I.S.&P. said I could feel free to pay *them* $39.95 a month
for the privilege of seeing freedom bleed out on my PC,
assured me I'd get my money's worth, that freedom would see to it.
The city infringed on Freedom's freedom to bind me.
I think I have to get more freedom if I wanna be free.

Freedom don't look good on my freedom,
see how it lies there, gashed through the body armor.
My freedom was in tech school, just welding, just HVAC.
My freedom had college ID but couldn't vote without a freedom permit.
The only thing freer than a gun with a bullet in the chamber
is the freedom pointing it at freedom.
Freedom breathes easier after it's loaded an AR-15.
Free to be bad assed, free to stand its ground.
Feel dat? All the heat and air
around an idea?
Freedom breathes like this-wishes somebody would
try to stop it from breathing the way it breathes.
The constitution of a semi-automatic's freedom
makes it easy to hyperventilate.

the cousin of death (after Sandy Hook)

Grandma's blanket cozied up around the neck,
thick blue socks,
the fray of a rose print patch
wisping white against hot skin.
I want sleep like this
that never leaves the couch
and falls like I never saw it coming,

to have such faith in waking up
I can catnap
while others work out my damnation.
The TV flickers and I wonder if you know
Duke Power charges for obliviousness,
that they don't discount
the wasted kilowatt hour.
I'm surprised, I thought you liked *Dexter*
and things are so tight nowadays,
we really can't afford tuning in to things
that can't keep our attention.

I get tired too. When somebodies say
being free means
getting used to the ghosts,
I get tired of listening.
When I reach for the lamp,
shake you to tell you about the boy
with the gun rack in his jacket,
what I hate about you
is the ugly face you make,
the pitiful scrunch of your cheekbones
like you've just swallowed something bitter.
I hate the don't shoot me hands you throw up
to block the flash of light.

The Blood (after Charleston)

I

We stack bodies at the fence by the road
in the Brady photos
faces grim with the need for the purge
twisted by the stench of lost cause
on their rotting flesh.

Solace our servitude with new miseries
we offer our blood for just that much
We pledge allegiance
to the peonage in the offing
to any flag but here.

II

Martin Viola and Medgar
Chaney Schwerner and Goodman
Ms. Cynt and Ms. Susie and Pastor
Twyanza and Doc and Sharonda
bulk up to take the shots
Reverend Simmons Ms. Ethel and Ms. Myra
pool and grow cool
around a Bible study table
die into the floor
at their bend in the circle
necks wrenched with the piercing
temples open
like the door of the church

They hung L.D. and Ms. Laura
from the bridge in Okemah
dangled them over the river like bait
celebrated the pendulous sway
of their desecrated bodies
in a photograph weighted by now
with timekeeping
We remember you

You are the heritage their heritage begets
We are a census of our stories
We can name names
before Charleston

III

Eulogize the wound in the wind
festoon every moment with self-deception
but not here
tell another lie
say the flag was sacrifice or blood money
acres or mules
anything like a tithe
on the value of breath
rally together for warmth
and flinch at regret in your back yards
but not here
where what we know
inoculates against nostalgia

IV

Forgiveness makes no demand
when it could. To be forgiven,
you must know the grace
of a discount.
You would have to believe
you were in debt.

the flag

my dad says
I told ya momma about that shirt.
she don't listen to nobody.

momma not political
so she really don't understand
she's not supposed to be wearing this little t-shirt
that says "southern girl"
with the confederate flag on it.

momma is a southern girl,
for sure. says she only wears it
in the yard tending to her flowers,
that she dug through a big bag of clothes
from ms. joan, sweet lady who keeps kids,

and that it fit her just fine. and it does.
momma looks right cute in it
if you don't think much.
we can't make her understand
she could be seen.

she would never approach ms. joan
about it, and if I see ms. joan,
I won't mention it.
ms. joan also gave her a book,
some Langston Hughes poetry

which I read to the babies.
If she just gone be out in the flowers,
I don't want to make a big deal.

Supremacy, or The Black Lifestyle

As much as *people* try to sound like they don't care, *some people* think a black president will look out for the black lifestyle. – woman from NC, on Ben Carson

I

Anything is possible here
this is no poverty of programming

no one compels
the holocaust in their volitions

the way they stud themselves with wifeys
poor babies they stroll about

petals they blow at the wind in idle time
that land where they land.

And these towers, austere
but sturdy, no worse

than what they've always known.
A quiet place to cull the herd.

II

black blood
courses with hemophilias
counts time in sickled cells
all manner
of heritable conditions
keloid the American skin

over the redline

my brother laid me down
says
fuck I look like, thinks

I should know better
than to come around
looking like something to eat

happened by
while he was
gaunt and emotional
bad lifetiming
find him
coached
always in pistol formation

my brother
crosses the street slow
wants you to hit him
mistakes his net worth
for his value
never was nettled
by planes and towers
wears his pants below his ass
like an accusation

III

you must be
a superhero
an overcomer   the way
you don't even come from
what you came from

just your
steely resolve, unbroken legs
and
joie de vivre
goading the want to
into
get-up-and-go
propelling you
toward pretentious subdivisions
Harris Teeters with wine bars

beyond beltways
even we aspire

to the charter school
beyond the terminus
of the MARTA line

IV

perhaps I can borrow

your imperviousness

can I

have it retroactivated

some

radical

reconstruction

at least

an EMT

who knows

how we bleed
in the absence
of clotting agents

while we can see the gauze
in each other's eyes

before my mouth

freezes in applause

and I gurgle more liberty
over the corners
of my lips

which are angled in your direction
like greater-than signs.

light reading

everybody comes for the waves,
the stripes on the rented umbrellas
all run the same way, their walls
are too sheer to keep secrets.

now she pats the chair to
"give me just a little more time"
as the surf swirls in
a shush under the play of grandbabies
their bowled bellies making molds
in tight one-piece suits—
breezes lift the blue frills, pink tails
would bloom with laughter
just over that water line
up and down this patch of beach
all day if they'd let 'em.

He keeps a thumb in the book
to hold a place,
reaches for the minus sign
on the speaker, says
Ma, check this out
low and somber,
like chatter in the pew.
Listen.

He reads but she's busy being glad
the baby is beyond the gauntlet of hot sand,
standing where she can cool bare feet.
He wonders aloud
Do you understand it?
He's coming out to...

but she cuts him off,
says *What would your daddy...*
and then stares over the romp of the beach,
fumbles for something
in the wrong purse.

How…?
She starts again, expelling the air,
shaking her head stylishly
beneath her straw hat.
I don't know Ma, he says,
it's somethin'—
then the water seeps away again,
caught in the act,
and the sun leans in close.
Anyone out of the water
is riveted with sweat.

Daddy vs. the National Longitudinal Lesbian Family Study

Tell you what son,
Go down there to that school, get that diploma and a job
and leave the rest of that mess down there.
It's crazy, it's crazy I don't see it and I ain't gone see it.
Folk down there don't know they butt
from a hole in the ground.
They ain't gone tell me I'm crazy.

When we stop needing mommas and daddies?
When that happen? Tell me son.
Why we got different parts and hormones and all that?
Last days, last days! Folk strain at a gnat
and swallow a camel. What you taking, a class?
They got a seminar on this sh—

Lord forgive me. Boy!
Got me 'bout to cuss.
UmmUMM!
Lord Jesus. Going to hell in a handbasket.
Turn the game on,
see what my Panthers doing.
Need no damn study.
Ain't none of y'all old enough
to piss off yaself.

Ain't gone make me feel bad
daddy got something to say to you
momma couldn't say. Ya hear?
And don't you let them make you feel bad,
you hear me? You ain't no bad person.

I ain't no bad person. I ain't crazy.

Ya momma ain't crazy.
They crazy.

They can pass whatever law they wanna pass
sky can be purple they want it to
but the day they say I gotta think crazy
I'm going to jail. You hear me?

Turn my game up now. Turn it up a 'lil mo.
Right there, ok, right there. Got me hot.
You know it's a lotta smart dumb niggas in the world don't ya?
Ok then. Come on now,
we need to do something with this ball dadgummit.
Come on Cam now,
let's go.

The wrong side of history

We couldn't prove it in court,
it wasn't like anything you could do a study on
stack up like witty stickers on a trunk hatch

or pretty frames for newfangled degrees
and their fancy watermarks,
nothing we could use as proof

the way a few years of W-2's
with full-figured end-of-year columns
was proof you could raise kids.

We vise-gripped what we knew,
tried to squeeze what we were thinking

into something unassailable and pithy
but it came out messy,
sounded mean

the way saying *no*
to anyone can sound mean.
We hadn't considered the alternatives

or contrived alibis for an ideal,
but then so many people were breathing
without mothers or fathers,

their survival was more proof, see
most of us believe we've turned out fine
so hatches couldn't be battened.

They said gimme
until righteousness meant
you'd be patient with acronyms,

until bewilderment
was the unpardonable sin,

and even the judge
said our paw-paws
tended intolerant collard greens,

that our big mamas
made bigoted biscuits.

Esoterica

I can teach him to walk and stand/ but he needs you/ to help him be a man – Jill Scott, "We Need You"

when you talk to me
talk like you talk to a sky
you need to unblue

come outside in the courtyard
and exegete

go slow over the part about
whatever being a man means

how delineation
leaves you disoriented—

tell us about what's called *patriarchy*
with particular attention
if you would

to how it circumscribes
the space between a woman's femur
and her tibia

gives her anterior cruciate ligament
its proclivity for shearing

illumines her skin in calcium.

Please, a defining of terms in the corpus

lest there be a question
in the back
there, in the back

a *cisgender* cista.
cis hard, cis crazy
out in these streets. cissy houston.
cis the most
wonderful time of the year. cis
boombah.

Jill said *we need you*
and we said
sang girl

we took it
how we take it

We watch Bill and Oprah and Iyanla
the daddyless daughters
the fatherless sons

and dab at our old-fashioned eyes.

Respectability

This old, bespectacled white man sits in the chair, faces straight ahead in his black dickies and green hooded team sweatshirt. He has a little brown bag lunch in the seat beside him and his hands are in grooves worn into his thighs. A couple seats back, two black girls start cussin', loud enough for me to hear, where I'm sitting in front of the white man, slanted toward the aisle. "*Oh he got me fucked up, nigga got me real fucked up. They saying he gotta do six months. Six months.*" She laughs that "ain't this some shit"-type laugh. So the other girl says "*Really? That's some bullshit,*" lower but audibly, as if to keep pace w/her friend's cussin'. The white man kinda turns and looks briefly, puts his hands back in the grooves, pulls paper out of the hand warmers on the hoodie, some list perhaps, puts it back, 'cause he knows better. It'll be over soon. I look at 'em. They don't notice that they're so noticeable. Why do I notice? Someone has to make you notice yourself and we're all afraid to do it. There's power in not noticing and we all know it, the white people know it, all these black people here that have that different shade of brown to 'em the closer we get to downtown, they know it. A brotha had just said *fuck that nigga* at the press conference after a game in front of white people and I was still mad. But my man said: you not responsible. They responsible. For all this shit. And he right. He say you madder at young bruh than them, which was some bullshit to say. I know if they didn't want us to cuss on the light rail, they shoulda made a different world. I read, nigga. I just don't know that if I call white man out he'll vote Democrat. And real talk I don't wanna look at this plain ass white man as culprit, as devil though I know he's responsible, a beneficiary. Either way, no matter how responsible he is, these girls are my responsibility. Right? I could say something he couldn't say. They my job, they belong to me. But why risk it. It'll be over soon. Me and the white man turn our heads like we synchronized. We look out at Minneapolis through the same window.

Boom Boom

when a lovely flame dies/smoke gets in your eyes—The Platters

Late nights
I'd be done whipped him
in Madden or PGA Golf
and he'd always be like
I 'bout had yo butt dat time,
then he'd go to the bathroom mirror
to bust Agent Orange bumps.

He used to smoke them Vantages,
light one up and sit on the toilet,
take a drag then hold it out
looking at it like it tasted new.
He'd squint through the smoke
and look at that thang like
yeah man, knew I knew that ass
from somewhere.

Father's Figure

honor roll

I think he must've kissed me on the lips in 8th grade on awards day. When he left, Chad said *"y'all still do that?"* and now I'm thinking he wouldn't have said that had Daddy just kissed me on the cheek.

hurl

I looked up from the toilet and he was leaned against the bathroom doorway, fist fixed at his hip. He was a halfhearted Samaritan, had come by in his tighty-whities and bypass scar to assess the damage.
Boy, you put meat on ya stomach
if you gone do that stuff.

run the streets

Have fun! Don't let me see you on the news, don't make me have to come ID you. Stay home sometime son. You ain't got to run to that girl house every day. You ain't got to be doing nothing. You hear me? Honey I ain't worried about you. I'm worried about them.

some

who do you take a thing like
man, you sho' know a lotta slow jams to not get no pussy to?
Given a choice between him
and Mom's guilt trips for a neglected Bible,
her soft hugs for crying spells I couldn't explain,
I chose *Shit, cha can't eat by yaself?*
Sound like you need some new friends.
Son, you gone turn out a lot better
than all these little boys you wanna be—
and when I looked into his eyes,
a question in my gaze,
he gathered me in, laughing,
his rough hands
squeezing the back of my arms.

Oh hush boy, he said.
Y'all in SUCH
a hurry.

Mornings, 1984

My daddy was an aspiration.
When he peed and how he prayed
I thought
well, that's never gone happen.

women

Boy I didn't know I was married 'til y'all came. ain't nuttin in them streets baby. they all made the same way. let me tell you, they all got the same...look, I know. they come out with a new model every day. Lord knows. Ya momma keep talking, mess around i'mma trade her in. ya hear me?

Ain't 'bout no sex. ya momma wonderful. I thank God for her every day. but you think this about sex? you know ya momma. she's a great mother. it ain't about that. she sweet as she can be, love her to death. I wish she was more outgoing, the business and all, you know I'm a talker. that ain't ya momma, just the way it is. and I know she wish I was a lot of things. but it ain't about us. it's about y'all. what Tina Turner say? what love got to do wit' it? there it is Whoop. ain't that what y'all say? go get yo' butt somebody and sit down somewhere. ain't nothing in these streets but babies and crabs.

Lenny

I won't ever leave you baby
I wanna begrieve you baby

"Are you saying begrieve?"
"Yep."
"That's not a word."
"I think it's a word."
"I don't think so."

"You know that gal you be having in that back room?"
"She got a name Daddy."
"Wait 'til y'all go ya separate ways. You don't know the word 'cause you don't know nothing 'bout it yet."

I won't ever leave you baby
I wanna begrieve you baby

Centenary A.M.E. Zion Church, Lilesville, NC

In time, you'd get used to the excitement of Wednesday night Bible study. Six or seven of the faithful would show and get treated to intermissions of my daddy or Uncle Jerry pulling kids out from under pews by the ankles. They took us to the tree arcing over the pastor's study, popped butts or stung our legs red with switches they wrenched loose in the moment when they hadn't already come prepared. At least it wasn't Granddaddy, him and that legendary fan belt off his '54 Pontiac—Daddy and Uncle Jerry were *progressive*. Anyway, they'd come back in and get right back into Ezekiel 37 like it was nothing. All the adults waited there patiently.

daddy

I remember my smallness in his lap,
the stench of Magic cream a necessary evil,
the smell of Brut washing away sin.

work

Daddy was a lot of folks' "inshonce" man, as they'd say down home—hustled from morning to past our bedtimes, ushered and eldered, smoked a lot and did it so long Momma started baking the chicken to ward off bypass surgery, so we all had to suffer. The bypass did in the smoking but he secreted plenty country ham in the crannies of the fridge over the years, fried it up in that black skillet at night for snacks over ColecoVision and Genesis. It got him but by then all the constancy I needed in the world I'd gotten every night around 11, from the rattle of a '79 Celica.

"you were meant for me" - donny

Science says Daddy was accidental flesh,
that there are no missions, no destiny,
that he wasn't meant for me.
But Daddy was no accident,
no random amalgam of flesh and bone
molded and melded by testosterone.
There was his procreative valence,
his way in the world,
and the right pinch of spice
at the curdling points.

the drop

The Applebee's hadn't settled yet but he figured he'd do half tonight, get from
Gainesville to Savannah and crash. He lit up, said *What if we leave now boy, gone
and hit this road*, looked out over the room from the fake wooden table, his feet
propped on its other chair. Momma sucked in air like a bad hiccup, cried the
way Momma cries right before you go fight whoever made her cry like that. But
Daddy was thinking about missing money. A tear rolled down his eye and he
took a drag from his Vantage, blew out the smoke like a movie.

When we got back to the dorm, the grey air barely swayed the palm trees. We
wiped our faces, I girded up in the back seat to leave but nobody was watching.
People milled about and two slight, shirtless white boys in khaki shorts and
backwards hats played hackeysak by the dorm entrance. I jumped out, waved at
Momma, and started walking.

Sunset in Huntersville

This pic catches the light piercing his eyes,
they're half-closed to diminish the glare,
he's turned toward the lake
as two rusty boys
blur into a race at the shoreline.
He shades his gaze
toward the specter
of the power plant.

And there's one with us up on his shoulders,
his blue shorts too high up his thighs,
white socks rimmed blue then yellow
too far up the calves,
our fingers like talons
clench and cave in his neat fro.
No straining, we waver
but he keeps us poised,
facing the camera.

The grass is a dark, veracious green
tapered neatly beneath a Carolina frisbee
that rests a few seconds
before the TCB on our hands
and the torque in our ashy elbows
send it back out under sunset.

Windsor Park (Welcome to Charlotte East)

Luxury

Here, it is 70 degrees in April no matter what you hear about Aleppo
and there are loose boards on my deck I don't wanna fix
that I can pay a handyman to replace

so even if the mosques they bomb date from the 8th century
two houses over
a neighbor watches two big dogs run around his yard
the white one occasionally pushing and mounting the grey one
each trying to get at the throw toy first.
their barks echo between the gaps in the houses,
pock the eardrum
like gunfire in the souq.

at Al-Nuqtah
the mosque of the drop of blood
Husayn's children spill blood
until no one can discern Husayn's drop
and I have the man come out to seed and aerate
so while there are greener yards than mine in this subdivision,
there aren't many.

Tranh's restaurant is next to Ali Baba's
El Copan shares the strip with Sheba
a Burger King is thrown in for the timid
up on Sharon Amity.
The Catholics and Methodists
suffer each other's edifices
and everyone wears the reds and blues
of their precepts
with impunity.

spontaneous generation

even the scientists will teach her
that maggots don't come out of old meat,
that some nasty fly planted a seed.
we are afraid she will think she made herself,
that she will be arrogant,
so we teach her to pray to someone big enough
to make worlds men can't make.
we want her peerless, and humble.

at bedtime she always kneels,
so pious even when I stand by
too tired to stoop,
wearied more by her role playing,
how it stretches bedtimes
like when she insists I be Moses
as she plays the bush.
she'll scooch down to where I am
and start the prayer over,
grab on to my leg
and hold on.

Sundays on Rosehaven

All day long, that thick black hair
had been impervious to the April breeze,
And the ruckus in the earphones
made for an easy mark.
So she crept toward the corner,
twirled into an alibi
as soon as she snatched at the plait,
Pitched toward the street so fast
cuidados were caroled from the bus stop,
Where men sipped muffled bottles
in paper bags.

And when she trained all the sass
of her whirl and stomp at the bench,
the full flop of her red hair bow
and the arms braided in attitude
in their general direction,

She was still too close to the curb,
too clever to care about traffic.

Cankerworms (for South Sudan)

better that the catkins were culprits,
how softly they fell to the ground
quiet as secrets, nothing to say
they would be there in the morning.
that first year,
the sky crackled a chorus of tiny maws
eating daylight into tree leaves,
and what fell into our eyes
as we searched for the sound
was the black buckshot
covering the cars.

if they get past the sticky traps
they will be slaves to their natures,
still gluttonous, clogging the gutters,
the stench of their stale rain
seeping through screen doors,
windows opened for spring air.
next year, there is the toxin
for the survivors, some atonal spray,
for we can assume that swelling
into song again, every year
the Lord brings.

Nesting

Evolution is a slow God. All the rain is weird lately, I swear it's warm too early, it's just a feeling. Six years in and now the birds decide to build a nest on the sill —we can't sleep, their wailing "*woodoos!*" come every morning just before six, too loud for blackout curtains, bleeding through our locked windows. The last two Aprils, the peach tree has bloomed pink on one thick branch, the others reach out desolate, as if smitten. Maybe it just needs some ammonium, or maybe the parasites have gotten to it. I'm pretty sure its something I'm not doing.

who needs 'im

I thought it'd be ok
to watch them sigh
through the crack in the door
as they ease into relapse.
I am here
to see what I'm doing.

There was the lingering over toys at bedtime,
how I clapped and barked in my deepest voice
until furniture moved,
all the air I take into lungs
the size of the strength I need
for cradling, the scoop and tote
from a cheap SUV
after sleep-sodden arrivals,
so they wake up tucked
and snug.

At first though,
her lilting whispers over naptimes,
and how she'd brush stroke
their pink heart lips,
gradually into latching.

Interventionism

We jumped on the Obama thing
because who really has 20 percent,
bought an older one for space
between the houses.
Probably go the magnet route
and hope we hit the lottery,
Folks live around here now
don't know the language.

But we love how loud the birds are,
even this far behind city lines.
And in April,
the pink blossoms on our peach tree
fall just like they would anywhere else,
just a heck of a lot closer
to the stadium.

Bad Haiku Workshop

the fewer descendants
of slaves you have to deal with,
the better the school.

without slavery
all the schools would be good—'stime
we acknowledged this.

when we say good school
we mean a school unburdened
by slave progeny.

a good school is one
with very few descendants
of African slaves.

the school unburdened
by the descendants of slaves
is called a "good school."

I send my kids to
good schools where there are very few
descendants of slaves.

Love, Changes (after Kashif)

I saw Tish on Central with some girl
one-handin' the stroller
'bout to run off a curb w/lil' man

had her finger danglin' over the canopy
trying to let him grab it.

Friend was hunchin' up her jeans,
pulling down the brim on her Bulls hat,
starin' at all of us in the cars
like what.

Then she palmed Tish ass
through the back pocket,
they kinda looked at each other,
smilin', squintin' and shit
through the sunlight
Ol' girl buttoned the top of Tish jacket.

Then they were walkin'
she was finessin' that ass looking at us
strokin' and scratchin' through the pocket
lookin' 'bout like Ty

when he was in there.

Upon the Passing of James Ingram

I played "One Hundred Ways" on my phone
and we sad-swayed a minute
but then she looked up and said
you know this is a me-too song
and I said how?
and she said
how about that she owes you a debt part?
and I said clearly you haven't listened to the lyrics
'cause if I got you wearing moonlight and pick you out a star

(nope, she said)

and it's *one more star*
meaning a star has been previously procured

(stop it)

this ain't regular dinner and a movie expectations

(hush)

and I said just give me some sugar
and she said negro
I'm as likely to get moonlight
and a couple stars for my own damn self as you are
and I said
please don't let them folks ruin a good dern song

A Favor

From here, we see you coming. I'm helpless, lost in the motion I love your momentum, so fascinated by each revolution, by what you accrue. This means you can't stay on task, I understand, there's gravity through every breath, such weight, the rolling, wheels within wheels, minds perpetually scattershot, rush-houred with thought, graced into destiny. God, you're special. When you arrive, sing my praises, know that I have not done often what your mother would never do, her genes addled needfully by instinct and custom. We were here, you wouldn't know what it's like to be heedless of all manner of permission and conquest, what can you know of the pleasures we set aside for the dream, the principles staid and stultifying which ennoble and sustain, that outlive the sudden deaths. Oh Splendor, only weapons of your own making can prosper, there are no devils. Marry someone who knows how to barter, knows that they must learn to forget. See that they have a bit of venom and a plain vision— photo albums are imperiled. When you choose, hear the clockwork jangle of my belt beyond the door, the bass of the hardwoods under my heavy traipse. Know who is wrong by their confidence in other ways. Remember these words, and the kiss goodnight, now onward forever, ever after the power and glory. I hope you will miss me but be wise and maybe I am never going anywhere.

A Foolish Consistency

Every week, on the way to our balcony pew
we'd catch a glimpse of this older guy
through the glass in the classroom door,
helping out in children's church.

He'd be leading a song with the first graders
or passing out snacks to preschoolers,
his all-weather short-sleeve button-ups or polos
tucked tightly over his paunch,

and once the sermon started he'd come in,
walk right up to this older lady
who'd always be there
manning a camera or spotlight,

and touch the small of her back
until she turned perfectly
into his quick kiss.

My wife would grab my leg as he approached
and I'd nod at the girls to look over
just to see the little one scrunch up her face,
just to see the oldest one smile.

Siege Mentality

Not now, not now,
not while my lips stink
and I smell of gas and grass,
before I stare too long at that knock
in that underwear below that t-shirt
and they notice me looking.
That sugar you offering is a reward
for something I do that you don't, and
we don't want them thinking
they can't weed whack.

Living like this
asserts into existence
a world. Any routine
is an agenda.
I really should have you out in this yard
at least every two or three cuts
around something besides the pansies
'cause we teach 'em somethin' baby,
when I'm up on the ladder
we insinuate purposes,
you moppin' and Swiffin' and cookin'
and me looking on
then making my lil' tea,
remembering the trash,
doing the dishes
to be useful.

Maybe as close as we'll get to a sweet by-and-by
where the wolf lies with the lamb
and the babies play with the snakes
is you taking out the trash
and me throwing some tilapia in the toaster oven,
beating y'all home some days
to gag myself through the feel
of raw meat to have some burger patties
ready off the grill when y'all get here.
Already the little one says

boys can't wear pink,
has never seen me in it,
yells *Mommy you can't do that!*
when you approach the driver's side,
like an oncoming truck
is careening through the windshield.

They interrupt football games to take orders,
empty the playroom fridge
to stack fake china with chewy bacon
and wafers of lettuce, tomatoes and peppers
petrified with plastic.
The other day,
I let them watch the girls kiss
on the Sam Smith video
like some kind of contingency plan,
the right side of history
and because we love the song,

they had said
"*oh my God! Daddy!*"
but I had imagined MacBooks atwitter
with lamentations in dissertations
for the American Girl dolls and playhouses,
the way we reek of sepia,
and maybe I went too far

so when you came in
I rushed over to grab the groceries,
to keep a finger on the scale
I kissed you too long
on the mouth.

Idolatry

something like a good luck ritual
his pressing into my skin,
the shade of muscadine wine
rushing toward the evidence of touch
like a greeting, his handprints
on my murmuring plush.
murmuring.

intentional eyes thrumming
altar call bedtimes
reverence me in the lamplight,
fingers fulcrum the grips
envisage my outline in the dark
a maven
each finger.

love marks impend
every night
a forensics of discipline
his ever-present obeisance
my wonder that he makes it
through the prayer.

Thank You Lord

The Chorus

Father we thank you for keeping us safe another day,
thank you for shelter and allowing us to see another day.
Lord we thank you for the girls,
help us to raise them the way you want us to,
bless our marriage, Lord bless this household.
We thank you for our jobs,
that we're able to pay bills
at a time so many others are less fortunate.
Father we pray for the people with loved ones overseas in war,
the innocent people who aren't even fighting,
that you comfort those families
that have lost loved ones.
Bless the President and his family Father,
help him to make wise decisions, good decisions
even if they aren't popular,
that our country might be blessed.
Lord we ask all these things in the name of your son Jesus,
Amen.

The Solo

Even though I have too much house for a liberal arts degree
and my deck extends too far into my back yard
and my school loan debt exceeds my yearly income
Lord I just wanna thank you for everything we have Father,
I just wanna thank you because we don't deserve our problems,
because it could be a lot worse,
because we don't deserve it but you do it anyway—
Father forgive me for cleaning the gutters today
and watching Elevation on TV instead of goin' on in,
I just wanna be a good steward of all that you've blessed me with
though I know I could've done them during the Panthers game,
Father show me how I can make amends
though I ask that they not be made by my attendance
at the father-daughter campout
or the men's fellowship meeting next Saturday,

Lord you know I'll be the only black guy,
and Father I'm not sure 'bout these Southern Baptists,
I like the facilities and the day care
but they ain't like A.M.E. Zionists Lord,
and plus the girls will be at Mom's for the weekend
and me and the wife been meaning to hit up that brunch at Zeta Jane's
and even if we skip Sunday
you know young white folks don't go to church
so you gotta get there early

Lord I know it's all grace and no deed is good enough
but maybe when the Witness lady comes
I can say something to make her believe
we're really on the same team,
that if you were that picky about names God help us,
if I can pull that off it should count,

Father thank you for our jobs
though you know we want different jobs,
Lord we pray for the President,
that you would give him wisdom and patience,
that you would move on them people's heart up there Lord
to help him give people more jobs, bless Michelle,
Lord I know it can't be easy,
bless the girls and Ms. Robinson…

Father I thank you

…Lord for integration,
how it's made me comfortable using words like *awesome* and *like* excessively
allowing me to assimilate at the job
and now Lord for my wife,
her hugs and cooked food, her thrifty obsessions,
the Goodwill and consignment shop trips,
the eBay and Craig's List stalking,
Lord for the blind spots, for her patience
and expertise with strong hair

and Father I thank you for the girls, that they belong to you,
that they are here for your will and your purpose

89

not just because we wanted to see what they'd look like
though that was part of it,
that I get to see the joy and the cute they exude
when they eat dollar menu ice cream cones,
thank you Father, they are so perfect
with little foreheads that meld into their eyebrows
and eyelashes like they 'sposed to, like you planned it
the bright whites of their fearfully and wonderfully made eyes
the contours of their cheeks and nostrils,
Glory to your name Father for how
no pic of them I've ever Facebooked
has gotten less than like, 23 likes Father,
for when I posted the pic of Z sleeping the other day
and it got 40 likes and Sosha said
"this pic makes my heart happy"
and I thought "you have no idea"
which is just a thing people say,
probably a cliché I learned in integration
and I kinda think she does know
even if she doesn't go to church.
Father we thank you for everything,
for sending your Son,
your will be done in our lives,
in the name of your son Jesus we pray,
Amen.

Genesis (for Na'im & Brittany)

who have I ever known better than you,
who on earth do I need besides you,
what great thing did I ever do
that you were not there to see?

how long has God planned this peace
fashioned this fit in His imaginings for us—
when I am in your arms
I hate that you were ever not mine to feel,
shudder at the thought
there were days you weren't here,
some days I am grieved
even by the time it took
to be prepared and primed

I was learning and working
believing some better version of me
would end at the best kind of you,
praying I was about His business in this world
seeking to be as pleasant in His eye
as you are in mine—
and look at God,

won't He furnish the evidence
of what we cannot see
so that we are changed by love
in a weekend,
who knew I'd be up the road
and find someone from down the way,
don't you just look familiar when you come around,
everybody lovin' on you like you belong to us,
like you were lost and found,
the family killed fatted calves
when I brought you home
to celebrate the end
of my wilderness

I love the Lord,
the routine of His astonishments,
the morning joy intensities
of His moderate moves,
the story of how you came to stand beside me
to share the good news of a good thing
in the presence of His people.
Father I thank you,
for I do believe in travail
I do not pretend
you have not brought me here for sacrifice
that the calling is not high
that the duty is not great
but I have come for the cleaving,

I thank you for the yoke
of this warm embrace
the easy burden of light in these eyes

and from now on
together we move from zenith to zenith
from this moment
to the potential energy of generations without end

but before the veil is lifted,
while this train
fills the courts of His temple,

Love I bring you my vows with sobriety,
promise to remember who I was
before your rain came,
that you are a blessing bespoken by grace,
for I know there are days to come
that we will forget what we were in the beginning
so menaced by the valleys
we don't notice the lilies—
and so I plight my troth

to be astounded every now and again
that I have the rest of my days
to countenance my complement,

to wonder sometimes at how
you were sent in my unworthiness
so that we might press together daily
toward the mark.

Notes

...And this I say, lest any man should beguile you with enticing words. - Colossians 2:2-4

Bayard Rustin, qtd in Long, Michael G. *Martin Luther King Jr., Homosexuality and the Early Gay Rights Movement*. New York: Palgrave Macmillan, 2012.

Bill Fletcher, Jr., qtd. in Amy B. Dean's "A Bigger Tent." *Boston Review*. 2 Feb. 2015. (http://www.bostonreview.net/books-ideas/amy-dean-richard-trumka-labor-movement)

"Unspeakable Realities Block Universal Health Coverage In America." *Forbes*. 13 Mar 2017. https://www.forbes.com/sites/chrisladd/2017/03/13/unspeakable-realities-block-universal-health-coverage-in-the-us/#5c901bf6186a

luh' friends

It's been a long time/I didn't think I was going to see you again/See you haven't changed/It's good to see you anyway- Cherelle and Alexander O'Neal, "Saturday Love"

"Heterosexism." *Merriam Webster Online*. (http://www.merriam-webster.com/dictionary/heterosexism)- discrimination or prejudice by heterosexuals against homosexuals

"Microaggression." *Dictionary.com*. (http://dictionary.reference.com/browse/microaggression)

1. a subtle but offensive comment or action directed at a minority or other nondominant group that is often unintentional or unconsciously reinforces a stereotype: *microaggressions such as "I don't see you as black."*

2. the use of such subtle but offensive comments or actions: *The diversity committee discussed the issue of microaggression toward women on campus.*

PrEP

"Pre-Exposure Prophylaxis." *Wikipedia: The Free Encyclopedia.* Wikimedia Foundation, Inc. (https://en.wikipedia.org/wiki/Pre-exposure_prophylaxis)

"Pre-Exposure Prophylaxis (PrEP)" *Centers for Disease Control and Prevention.* (http://www.cdc.gov/hiv/risk/prep/index.html)

Chappell, Terrence. "PrEP and Beyond: HIV/AIDS & Black, Gay Men." *EBONY.* 26 Oct. 2015. (http://www.ebony.com/wellness-empowerment/prep-and-beyond-hivaids-black-gay-men-567#ixzz3z1I7GVgO)

Distraction (Harmony, In Red)

"Harmony in Red: Lamplight." James Abbott McNeill Whistler - The Complete Works, www.jamesabbottmcneillwhistler.org/Harmony-In-Red-Lamplight.html.

Spew.

Luke 9:57-62 (KJV)

Predestination

"North Carolina Highlights." *AIDSVu.org.* (http://aidsvu.org/state/north-carolina/)

not my will

Friedman, Richard. "Infidelity Lurks in Your Genes." *New York Times.* 22 May 2015. (http://nyti.ms/1c9wfqe)

"So do we get a moral pass if we happen to carry one of these "infidelity" genes? Hardly. We don't choose our genes and can't control them (yet), but we can usually decide what we do with the emotions and impulses they help create. But it is important to acknowledge that we live our lives on a very uneven genetic playing field… For some, there is little innate temptation to cheat; for others, sexual monogamy is an uphill battle against their own biology."

James, Susan Donaldson. "Thrill-Seeking Gene Can Lead to More Sex Partners." *ABC News.* 6 Dec 2010. (http://abcnews.go.com/Health/scientists-discover-gene-responsible-cheating-promiscuous-sex-habits/story?id=12322891)

"In what is being called a first of its kind study, researchers at Binghamton University, State University of New York (SUNY) have discovered that about half of all people have a gene that makes them more vulnerable to promiscuity and cheating.

Those with a certain variant of the dopamine receptor D4 polymorphism—or DRD4 gene—"were more likely to have a history of uncommitted sex, including one-night stands and acts of infidelity," according to lead investigator Justin Garcia.

DRD4 is the "thrill-seeking" gene, also responsible for alcohol and gambling addictions. The gene can influence the brain's chemistry and subsequently, an individual's behavior.

The desire to cheat or sleep around seems to originate in the brain's pleasure and reward center, where the "rush" of dopamine motivates those who are vulnerable, the researchers say.

In the study, Garcia instructed 181 student volunteers at SUNY to take an anonymous survey on their previous sexual behavior, asking them questions like how many sex partners they had and if they had ever been unfaithful.

He then tested their DNA by oral rinsing with a special mouthwash...and genotyped the DRD4.

His team discovered that there is a variation in the thrill-seeking gene and those with much longer alleles are more prone to, well, getting prone. (An allele is part of the gene's DNA sequence responsible for different traits such as eye color or curly hair.)

Those with at least one 7-repeat allele reported a higher rate of promiscuity that is, admitting to a "one-night stand." The same group had a 50 percent increase in instances of sexual cheating.

"It turns out everyone has got the gene," said Garcia, who is a doctoral fellow in the laboratory of evolutionary anthropology and health at SUNY Binghamton. "Just as height varies, the amount of information in the gene varies. In those who have more, their alleles are longer and they are more prone to thrill-seeking."

"It's inheritable, too," he said. "If your parents have it, you have it."
When the brain is stimulated—drinking alcohol, jumping from planes, having sex — it releases dopamine, the pleasure response hormone…

But not everyone is convinced a roving eye is rooted in DNA.

"Certain people are vulnerable to affairs, but in the end, it's about personal choice," said Jenn Berman, a psychotherapist and host of "The Love and Sex Show" on Cosmo Radio. "And it depends on how well-developed their impulse control is."

Still, the study could have some interesting implications.

Armed with that kind of data, John Coleman said he might be inclined to test his fiancé and himself as well.

"It's like getting tested for STDs," he said. "It's the ultimate form of honesty, really," he said…"

Belluck, Pam. "In Study, Fatherhood Leads to Drop in Testosterone." *New York Times*. 12 Sep. 2011.
(http://www.nytimes.com/2011/09/13/health/research/13testosterone.html?_r=0)

Szalavitz, Maia. "Is It Possible to Create an Anti-Love Drug?" *New York Magazine*. 19 May 2014. (http://nymag.com/scienceofus/2014/05/anti-love-drugs-will-change-how-we-end-romances.html)

Yancy, George, bell hooks. "bell hooks: Buddhism, the Beats and Loving Blackness." *New York Times*. 10 Dec 2015.
(http://opinionator.blogs.nytimes.com/2015/12/10/bell-hooks-buddhism-the-beats-and-loving-blackness/?_r=0)

"...one of the reasons for why so much black rebel anti-racist movements failed is because they didn't take care of the home as a site of resistance. So, you have very wounded people trying to lead movements in a world beyond the home, but they were simply not psychologically fit to lead."

Poetry Thug: kill nuttin' let nuttin' die (after Mobb Deep)

Mobb Deep. "The Infamous Prelude." *The Infamous*, RCA Records, 1995.

Gilmore, Brian. "What Baraka Was Really Saying." *Chocolate City Review*. 02 May 2013. (https://chocolatecityreview.wordpress.com/2013/05/02/what-baraka-was-really-saying/comment-page-1/)

Safe Space

Hicks, Tony. "Ellen DeGeneres and Pharrell talk Kim Burrell controversy." *The Mercury News*. 05 Jan. 2017. (http://www.mercurynews.com/2017/01/05/ellen-degeneres-and-pharrell-explain-kim-burrell-controversy/)

KillaBig3000. "Kanye West - Don't Stop (ft. Pharrell & Lupe Fiasco) {LYRICS+DOWNLOAD} HD." *YouTube*. 12 Oct. 2010. (https://www.youtube.com/watch?v=bxQXvruWJiwf)

Lyons, Patrick. "Future Says Pharrell Was Hesitant To Appear On 'Move That Dope.'" *HotNewHipHop*. 23 May 2014. (https://www.hotnewhiphop.com/future-says-pharrell-was-hesitant-to-appear-on-move-that-dope-news.10665.html)

Pirates

"All In With Chris Hayes, Wednesday, April 10th, 2013." *NBCNews.com*. (http://www.nbcnews.com/id/51542483/ns/msnbc-all_in_with_chris_hayes/)

hell you say

"'The Melissa Harris-Perry Show' for Saturday, July 7, 2012." NBCNews.com. (http://www.nbcnews.com/id/48121158/ns/msnbc/)

Harris-Perry: It feels there's always been a lot of queer in hip-hop...the homoeroticism of all my boys together, me and all my boys. Like there's no woman in the room, right?

Michael Eric Dyson: Yes, that's a great point, because the iconography of homosocial reality... is always there. Look, wearing your pants down to see your BVDs...an attempt within jail culture to signify who and whom cannot be touched. So in one sense, it's a transfer from gay culture without the acknowledgment and without the copyright and without the footnote, but also I think it`s the real challenge of hip-hop culture—to figure out a way to speak about masculinity and to include all of those different...expressions of masculinity. So, yes, in one sense, it's always been there right before our eyes... The church and hip-hop have a lot in common...A guy who says, I`m going out with 12 guys, Jesus and his 12 guys, my disciples over women, now this is my boys over women..."

Ross, Janell. "'White privilege' just made an appearance in the presidential race. It's about time." *Washington Post*. 12 Jan. 2016. (https://www.washingtonpost.com/news/the-fix/wp/2016/01/12/white-privilege-just-made-an-appearance-in-the-presidential-race-its-about-time/)

"...'white privilege' is one of those terms — like 'intersectionality,' 'rape culture' and the much-talked about 'microaggression' — that have escaped the academy and entered the mainstream. They are approaching widespread use among young people on the political left, due in large part to the sincere efforts of activists and academics who provide some kind of language to discuss and draw attention to issues that shape American life. They are also terms that many Americans not only don't really know but also instinctively don't trust or believe to be real. And the complexity and rarified nature of those words sometimes becomes the subject of distracting discussion when simple, clear language might have done more to advance a substantive debate."

"Benjamin ("Pitchfork") Tillman." *Wikipedia: The Free Encyclopedia*. Wikimedia Foundation, Inc. (https://en.wikipedia.org/wiki/Benjamin_Tillman)

"Intersectionality." *Dictionary.com*. 2016. (http://www.dictionary.com/browse/intersectionality)

1. the theory that the overlap of various social identities, as race, gender, sexuality, and class, contributes to the specific type of systemic oppression and

discrimination experienced by an individual (often used attributively):

Her paper uses a queer intersectionality approach.

2. the oppression and discrimination resulting from the overlap of an individual's various social identities:

the intersectionality of oppression experienced by black women.

"Bigot." *Merriam-Webster Online.* Merriam-Webster, 2016. (http://www.merriam-webster.com/dictionary/bigot)

Hofer, Jen. "If You Hear Something Say Something, Or If You're Not At The Table You're On The Menu." *Entropy.* 18 Dec. 2015. (http://entropymag.org/if-you-hear-something-say-something-or-if-youre-not-at-the-table-youre-on-the-menu/)

The Legend of Famous Jameis

Hanstock, Bill. "Jameis Winston stood on a table at FSU and yelled, 'F—k her right in the p—y'." *SBNation.com.* 16 Sep. 2014. (http://www.sbnation.com/lookit/2014/9/16/6252613/jameis-winston-stood-on-a-table-at-fsu-and-yelled-f-k-her-right-in)

Tread on Me

Stinson, Jeffrey. "Cities, States Face Off On Municipal Broadband." *The Pew Charitable Trusts.* 11 Aug. 2014. (http://www.pewtrusts.org/en/research-and-analysis/blogs/stateline/2014/08/11/cities-states-face-off-on-municipal-broadband)

…The core question is whether high-speed Internet access is such an economic necessity that municipal governments in less-populated areas of the country should provide it when private companies won't.

To advocates of municipal broadband, the answer is clear.

"It's something we have to have," said James Baller, a Washington, D.C., lawyer who specializes in municipal broadband issues and heads the Coalition for Local

Internet Choice. "The nations that have it will be the ones most successful in the emerging global economy."

Foes, including private Internet service providers such as Comcast, AT&T and Time Warner Cable, have a different view. They say they are spending hundreds of millions of dollars upgrading infrastructure to give high-speed access to every American, and that government shouldn't compete against private companies, which must pay taxes and make a profit.

"In general, we don't think municipalities should compete with private capital when their areas are served (by private providers)," said Sena Fitzmaurice, vice president of government communications for Comcast Corp., the nation's largest Internet service provider.

The Blood

McCoy, Terrence. "Darren Wilson Explains Why He Killed Michael Brown." *Washington Post.* The Washington Post, 25 Nov. 2014. (https://www.washingtonpost.com/news/morning-mix/wp/2014/11/25/why-darren-wilson-said-he-killed-michael-brown/)

Supremacy, or The Black Lifestyle

Peoples, Steve. "Carson Tells NASCAR Fans Confederate Flag is OK on Private Property." *Public Broadcasting Service.* 28 Sept. 2015. (http://www.pbs.org/newshour/rundown/carson-tells-nascar-fans-confederate-flag-ok-private-property/)

When I was comin' up rough/that wasn't even what you called it/that's why I smoke blunts now and run with alcoholics- Tupac, "F—k The World"

Martin, Dawn Lundy. "The Long Road to Angela Davis's Library." *The New Yorker.* 26 Dec. 2014. (http://www.newyorker.com/books/page-turner/long-road-angela-davis-library)

"What, in the end, is politicization? Is it when you recognize that things are wrong and unjust in the world, or is it when you understand how powerful the powers are that seek to prevent you from changing anything? We learn, over time, that social and political change is made so incrementally that the present can look exactly like the past..."

Monroe, Doug. "Where It All Went Wrong." *Atlanta Magazine*. 1 Aug 2012.
(http://www.atlantamagazine.com/great-reads/marta-tsplost-transportation/)

"Criminologist Believes Violent Behavior is Biological." *NPR*.
(http://www.npr.org/2014/03/21/292375166/criminologist-believes-violent-behavior-is-biological)

"I've got to be careful…There's no destiny here. Biology is not destiny, and it's more than biology, and there's lots of factors that we're talking about there, and one factor like prefrontal dysfunction or low heart rate doesn't make you a criminal offender. But what if all the boxes were checked? What if you had birth complications and you were exposed to toxins and you had a low resting heart rate and you had the gene that raises the odds of violence, et cetera… stuff happening early on in life. I mean, you're not responsible for that. Then how in the name of justice can we really hold that individual as responsible as we do ... and punish them as much as we do — including death?"

Daddy vs. the National Longitudinal Lesbian Family Study

Park. Alice. "Study: Children of Lesbians May Do Better Than Their Peers." *Time*. 7 Jun 2010.
(http://content.time.com/time/health/article/0,8599,1994480,00.html)

They

Wolf, Richard. "Gay marriage controversy focuses on children." *USA Today*. 28 Apr. 2015.
(http://www.usatoday.com/story/news/nation/2015/04/21/supreme-court-gay-marriage-children/25935489/)

Kurtzleben, Danielle. "Gay Couples More Educated, Higher-Income Than Heterosexual Couples." *USNews.com*. 1 Mar. 2013.
(http://www.usnews.com/news/articles/2013/03/01/gay-couples-more-educated-higher-income-than-heterosexual-couples)

"Women who are in same-sex couples and in the labor force tend to make far more money than similar women in heterosexual couples, while men in gay couples tend to make slightly less than their heterosexual counterparts. People in gay couples are also more likely to be in the labor force (that is, working or looking for a job) than their heterosexual counterparts, and they're far more likely to be highly educated.

Those are a few of the datapoints from a new report on the demographics of America's same-sex couples. The Williams Institute, a think tank at UCLA that focuses on LGBT issues, has dissected Census data from 2005 through 2011 to create a detailed picture of the demographics of men and women who live with people of the same sex...

Among same-sex couples with both partners in the labor force, median household income is significantly higher ($94,000) than among heterosexual couples ($86,000). That's likely due to a number of factors, but education is likely one of them, says Gary Gates, a distinguished scholar at the Williams institute and the study's author. Around 46 percent of people in same-sex couples have college degrees, compared to under one-third of people in heterosexual couples. That higher level of education also likely contributes to higher incomes for same-sex households..."

Regnerus, Mark. "Does It Really Make No Difference If Your Parents Are Straight or Gay?" *Slate*. 11 June 2012. (http://slate.com/human-interest/2012/06/gay-parents-are-they-really-no-different.html)

"...On 25 of 40 different outcomes evaluated [in the author's New Family Structures Study] the children of women who've had same-sex relationships fare quite differently than those in stable, biologically-intact mom-and-pop families, displaying numbers more comparable to those from heterosexual stepfamilies and single parents. Even after including controls for age, race, gender, and things like being bullied as a youth, or the gay-friendliness of the state in which they live, such respondents were more apt to report being unemployed, less healthy, more depressed, more likely to have cheated on a spouse or partner, smoke more pot, had trouble with the law, report more male and female sex partners, more sexual victimization, and were more likely to reflect negatively on their childhood family life, among other things. Why such dramatic differences? I can only speculate, since the data are not poised to pinpoint causes. One notable theme among the adult children of same-sex parents, however, is household instability, and plenty of it. The children of fathers who have had same-sex relationships fare a bit better, but they seldom reported living with their father for very long, and never with his partner for more than three years."

respectability

Travis, Clay. "Andrew Harrison during Frank Kaminsky Question: 'F— That N —'" *FOX Sports*. 05 Apr. 2015. (http://www.foxsports.com/college-football/outkick-the-coverage/andrew-harrison-on-frank-kaminsky-f-that-n-040415)

esoterica

"Patriarchy." *Merriam Webster Online*. (http://www.merriam-webster.com/dictionary/patriarchy) - social organization marked by the supremacy of the father in the clan or family, the legal dependence of wives and children, and the reckoning of descent and inheritance in the male line; broadly: control by men of a disproportionately large share of power

"Sexual dimorphism." *Wikipedia: The Free Encyclopedia*. Wikimedia Foundation, Inc. (https://en.wikipedia.org/wiki/Sexual_dimorphism)

"Sexual dimorphism is the condition where the two sexes of the same species exhibit different characteristics beyond the differences in their sexual organs themselves. The condition occurs in many animals, insects, birds and some plants. Differences may include secondary sex characteristics, size, color, markings, and may also include behavioral differences..."

"Human skin color." *Wikipedia: The Free Encyclopedia*. Wikimedia Foundation, Inc. (https://en.wikipedia.org/wiki/Human_skin_color)

"It has been observed that adult human females are consistently lighter in skin pigmentation than males in the same population. This form of sexual dimorphism is due to the requirement in human females for high amounts of calcium during pregnancy and lactation. Breastfeeding newborns, whose skeletons are growing, require high amounts of calcium intake from the mother's milk (about 4 times more than during prenatal development), part of which comes from reserves in the mother's skeleton. Adequate vitamin D resources are needed to absorb calcium from the diet, and it has been shown that deficiencies of vitamin D and calcium increase the likelihood of various birth defects such as spina bifida and rickets. Natural selection has led to females with lighter skin than males in all indigenous populations because women must get enough vitamin D and calcium to support the development of fetus and nursing infant and to maintain their own health.

"ACL Injuries: Female Athletes At Increased Risk." momsTEAM.com. (http://www.momsteam.com/health-safety/muscles-joints-bones/knee/acl-injuries-in-female-athletes)

"Definition of Cisgender in English." Oxford Dictionary. (http://www.oxforddictionaries.com/us/definition/american_english/cisgende r)-Denoting or relating to a person whose sense of personal identity and gender corresponds with their birth sex.

Blank, Paula. "Will 'Cisgender' Survive?" *The Atlantic*. 24 Sep. 2014. (http://www.theatlantic.com/entertainment/archive/2014/09/cisgenders-linguistic-uphill-battle/380342/)

Father Figures

"Anti-Mullerian hormone." *Wikipedia: The Free Encyclopedia*. Wikimedia Foundation, Inc. (https://en.wikipedia.org/wiki/Anti-M %C3%BCllerian_hormone)

"…In mammals, AMH prevents the development of the Müllerian ducts into the uterus and other Müllerian structures… In humans, this action takes place during the first 8 weeks of gestation. If no hormone is produced from the gonads, the Müllerian ducts automatically develop, while the Wolffian ducts, which are responsible for male reproductive parts, automatically die… In men, inadequate embryonal AMH activity can lead to the *Persistent Müllerian duct syndrome* (PMDS), in which a rudimentary uterus is present and testes are usually undescended. The AMH gene (*AMH*) or the gene for its receptor (*AMH-RII*) are usually abnormal. AMH measurements have also become widely used in the evaluation of testicular presence and function in infants with intersex conditions, ambiguous genitalia, and cryptorchidism (missing testis)…"

spontaneous generation

"Spontaneous generation." *Wikipedia: The Free Encyclopedia*. Wikimedia

Foundation, Inc. (https://en.wikipedia.org/wiki/Spontaneous_generation)

Cankerworms (for South Sudan)

"2014 Bentiu massacre." *Wikipedia: The Free Encyclopedia*. Wikimedia Foundation, Inc. (https://en.wikipedia.org/wiki/2014_Bentiu_massacre)

who needs 'im

Hampikian, Greg. "Men, Who Needs Them?" *New York Times*. 24 Aug 2012. (http://nyti.ms/1DJ3ibK)

""...women are both necessary and sufficient for reproduction, and men are neither. From the production of the first cell (egg) to the development of the fetus and the birth and breast-feeding of the child, fathers can be absent. They can be at work, at home, in prison or at war, living or dead...Then, at some point, your father spent a few minutes close by, but then left. A little while later, you encountered some very odd tiny cells that he had shed. They did not merge with you, or give you any cell membranes or nutrients — just an infinitesimally small packet of DNA, less than one-millionth of your mass..." -

"Amygdala." *Wikipedia: The Free Encyclopedia*. Wikimedia Foundation, Inc. (https://en.wikipedia.org/wiki/Amygdala)

"The amygdala is one of the best-understood brain regions with regard to differences between the sexes. The amygdala is larger in males than females in children ages 7–11, in adult humans, and in adult rats.

In addition to size, other functional and structural differences between male and female amygdalae have been observed. Subjects' amygdala activation was observed when watching a horror film and subliminal stimuli. The results of the study showed a different lateralization of the amygdala in men and women. Enhanced memory for the film was related to enhanced activity of the left, but not the right, amygdala in women, whereas it was related to enhanced activity of the right, but not the left, amygdala in men. One study found evidence that on average, women tend to retain stronger memories for emotional events than men.

The right amygdala is also linked with taking action as well as being linked to negative emotions, which may help explain why males tend to respond to emotionally stressful stimuli physically. The left amygdala allows for the recall of details, but it also results in more thought rather than action in response to emotionally stressful stimuli, which may explain the absence of physical response in women."

Upon the Passing of James Ingram

HiFiveVEVO. "Hi-Five - She's Playing Hard to Get." YouTube, 16 March 2014. (https://www.youtube.com/watch?v=LKLnifIvnDQ)

Idolatry

the *poweruice* was pure Brita water filter juice - MF Doom, "Rhymes Like Dimes"

Thank You

Father for your mercy, for sufficiency in my home, for everything I can't have that you know I can't handle, for the benevolence of your stumbling blocks. Help me to be useful and constructive.

Makia for your faith in me, your resilience, this family, all the little things I never see, and for pretending to be impressed just enough to make me want to keep at this. I love you. Rissy and Z—beautiful messes, the both of you. I love you and can't wait to see what you do in the world. I know I probably seem distracted a lot but please know I will cherish your hugs long after you want to lavish me with them the way you do now. Mom: Thank you for praying without ceasing. Daddy: I miss you terribly. And I know you're loving this (wink). Nana Little: Thank you for your daughter and the sustenance of your prayers. Na'im and Brittany—Thanks for "commissioning" "Genesis." The story of your love is an inspiration and proof that "they that wait upon the Lord shall renew their strength." Mr. Moses—thank you for your encouragement and faith. God bless you and Nana Moses. Katie Becker—I know right? Finally! Thanks for your encouragement and support. Florida fam-Tony/LB/Luke/D. Rizzle/Sco/Ant Banks/Wayniac-fuh life. Shante Bridges—you are a good friend. Thank you for keeping up with folks—love always. Dia Clemons—somehow I missed you last time. Thanks for your friendship and for the chocolate chip-less cookies. Business Wire (Matt Ashman, Casey Hann, Lisa Beth Scheibner)-thanks for being (involuntary) sounding boards for my ideas about so many of the articles that informed this collection. Willow Books-Heather Buchanan, big bro Randall Horton, Patricia Biela, Adrienne Christian (so dern proud of you), the prolific Curtis Crisler (thank you for teaching *Lilies*), Derrick "Scrippas" Harriell, Angie Chuang, Angela Narciso Torrez, April Gibson, Rachelle Escamilla (thanks for your generosity in having me on KKUP).

Cave Canem- Amanda Johnston: thank you for the invite to participate in NaPoWriMo in 2014. This book doesn't exist without that experience. I can't remember the whole group now, but I got to (cyber) meet Avery Young and have folks like Stacey Tolbert (anastacia renée) and Aricka Foreman provide input on the earliest poems. And Natalie Graham and Jonterri Gadson and Qiana Towns if I'm not mistaken (?)—I can't remember us all, but that month was like a fourth year of Cave Canem. Destiny Birdsong—thank you for being the first to teach *Lilies* and for allowing me the opportunity to share the stage with folks like Donika (Kelly) and Lamar (Wilson) in my first opportunity to read after the book came out. You have been a blessing and a good friend. Nicole Sealey—thanks for seeing fit to drop a country boy who'd never set foot in NYC before in the middle of a reading with the likes of Wendy Walters and Adrian Matejka. Thank you for all you did for many of us th rough Cave Canem. I know whatever work you put your hands to from here will be special. Reggie Harris: Thanks for the opportunity to read in Baltimore. Dr. Joanne Gabbin and Lauren K. Alleyne—thanks for all you do with Furious Flower (and for letting me eat with y'all after the readings.) To the Carolinas African-American Writers Collective—thank you Dr. L. Teresa Church, Grace Ocasio, Lenard Moore, Crystal Simone Smith, Sheila Smith McKoy, Angela Belcher-Epps, Diane Judge, Gideon Young—thank you all for your ear and input. Raina León: You are a great example on multiple levels-I appreciate your remarkable dedication to family, teaching, and writing.

To the kind and generous Carolinas poetry family that gave me space to read from and/or carried *Lilies In The Valley:* Park Road Books, Malaprops, Quail Ridge Books, Adah Fitzgerald and Catherine Hamilton-Genson at Main Street Books, Melissa Hassard, C.T. McGaha, Dr. Malin Pereira, Dr. Jeffery Leak, and Bryn Chancellor (UNCC, which set me on my way-#notonemore-Bryn thanks for letting me stand in for the gifted and underrated Quentin Talley), The Book Shelf, Joe's Place, McIntyre's Fine Books (Mr. Shelby Stephenson—a pleasure sir), Scott Owens of Poetry Hickory, the ubiquitous Jonathan Kevin Rice, Caleb Beissert of Asheville Poetry Series (what up Kevin Evans!), Ed Southern and Charles Fiore of the N.C. Writers Network, big brother Al Black and my man Len Lawson for the Poets Respond to Race Tour (appreciate you brother). Thanks to fellow readers/features: Bianca Diaz, Al Maginnes, John Lane, Coen Crisp, Janet Joyner, Sara Claytor (thank you for recommending me to Scott Owens), and Charmaine Cadeau Ward. To Elizabeth Barnett, Dr. Damaris Hill, Michael Broder, Karineh Mahdessian, and all the editors and readers who decided to share my work as well as all the readers at all the places that considered this manuscript. I am especially grateful for the encouragement I received from being a finalist or semifinalist for the poetry prizes at Cleveland State University, the University of Akron, Fresno State University, Pleaides, Press 53, and Saturnalia.

American University-Kyle Dargan (thanks for giving me occasion to read with and meet my AU kinfolk Abdul Ali and Jenny Molberg), Myra Sklarew (I can't believe you came in that weather), my wonderful '04 classmates that came out that night. Steve Castro—thanks for showing love and sharing my work.

Exit 4 ("I'm gonna love you for life"), Phonte and Foreign Exchange, J. Cole, Beyonce, Bill Maher, Jericho Brown ("Like Father"), Robin Coste Lewis, Kemba (gonna miss you dog), Bettina Judd, Skyzoo, Danez Smith, Phillip B. Williams, Steve Smith, L. Lamar Wilson, Cam (sometimes leaving G'ville is just the beginning-we need that ring fam), and Tamryn Spruill (I see you! Kill it!) for inspiration, conversation, edification, excellence, audacity and/or generosity. To the Facebook fam I stay stealing articles/insight from-Brian Gilmore, Ernesto Mercer, Nadir Lasana Bomani, Kenneth Carroll. Joseph Ross, my lone reviewer in the world-God bless you and thank you for your kindness in exposing people to my work for no reason and for giving Mom some poetry to like besides mine.

Pastor Howard-John Wesley: I believe you and Alfred Street were brought into our life for such times as these, for comfort during this sojourn from our home. You may never see this but thank you for speaking truth to power and for reminding us that the testimony is in our brokenness.

Venus Thrash-You hard on a brother but I love you. Thanks for your refining fire in this work. I know you're in my life for a reason. Kwoya—I will never forget you at Cave-you were the first person I met. I was wandering around, nervous, unsure of where to go and not wanting to ask. You grabbed my arm and said "Slow down! What. Is. Your. Name?" Thank you for taking time to slow down despite all you have going on to be another set of eyes for me. Dandan Luo—You are so talented and patient (and fly!) I can't thank you enough for bringing the vision for the cover to fruition. Alan Michael Parker—you are the man. Nobody B.S.s a blurb or reading intro like you. Thanks for doing both for me along the way. Jason McCall—when I read *Two Face God* I knew we were some kin. Thanks for taking the time.

WordTech: Kevin and Lori—thank you for your patience as I completed my run through the gauntlet of contests and most of all, for your confidence in me and this manuscript. I pray it will prove to be well founded.

Made in USA - North Chelmsford, MA
1030663_9781625493330
12.05.2019 1716